Dear Parent:
Your child's love of reading starts here!

Every child learns to read in a different way and at his or her own speed. Some go back and forth between reading levels and read favorite books again and again. Others read through each level in order. You can help your young reader improve and become more confident by encouraging his or her own interests and abilities. From books your child reads with you to the first books he or she reads alone, there are I Can Read Books for every stage of reading:

SHARED READING
Basic language, word repetition, and whimsical illustrations, ideal for sharing with your emergent reader

BEGINNING READING
Short sentences, familiar words, and simple concepts for children eager to read on their own

READING WITH HELP
Engaging stories, longer sentences, and language play for developing readers

READING ALONE
Complex plots, challenging vocabulary, and high-interest topics for the independent reader

I Can Read Books have introduced children to the joy of reading since 1957. Featuring award-winning authors and illustrators and a fabulous cast of beloved characters, I Can Read Books set the standard for beginning readers.

A lifetime of discovery begins with the magical words **"I Can Read!"**

Visit www.icanread.com for information
on enriching your child's reading experience.

*Visit www.zonderkidz.com/icanread for more faith-based
I Can Read! titles from Zonderkidz.*

> A message came to Jonah from the Lord ...
> He said, "Go to the great city of Nineveh.
> Announce to its people the message I give you."
> —*Jonah 3:1–2*

ZONDERKIDZ

Jonah, God's Messenger
Copyright © 2011 by Zondervan
Illustrations © 2011 by Dennis G. Jones

An **I Can Read Book**

Requests for information should be addressed to:
Zondervan, 3900 *Sparks Drive SE, Grand Rapids, Michigan* 49546

Library of Congress Cataloging-in-Publication Data

Jonah, God's messenger.
   p. cm. — (I can read!)
   ISBN 978-0-310-71835-2 (softcover)
   1. Jonah (Biblical prophet)—Juvenile literature.
   BS580.J55J62 2011
   224'.9209505—dc22   2010053408

Scriptures taken from the Holy Bible, *New International Reader's Version*®, NIrV®. Copyright © 1995, 1996, 1998 by Biblica, Inc.® Used by permission of Zondervan. All rights reserved worldwide.

Any internet addresses (websites, blogs, etc.) and telephone numbers printed in this book are offered as a resource. They are not intended in any way to be or imply an endorsement by Zondervan, nor does Zondervan vouch for the content of these sites and numbers for the life of this book.

No part of this publication may be reproduced, stored in a retrieval system, or transmitted in any form or by any means — electronic, mechanical, photocopy, recording, or any other — except for brief quotations in printed reviews, without the prior permission of the publisher.

Published in association with the literary agency of Alive Literary Agency, www.aliveliterary.com

Zonderkidz is a trademark of Zondervan.

I Can Read® and I Can Read Book® are trademarks of HarperCollins Publishers.

Editor: Mary Hassinger

Printed in Vietnam

JONAH
God's Messenger

pictures by Dennis G. Jones

Jonah was a prophet.

He loved God.

He told many people about God.

One day, God said to Jonah,

"Go to Nineveh.

It is a big city.

Tell the people to stop being bad."

But Jonah was not happy

about this job.

Jonah did not want to help those people.

He ran away.

He made a plan to go to Tarshish.

Tarshish was far away.

Jonah could not walk that far!

He bought a ticket

to go away on a boat.

God did not want Jonah
to go to Tarshish.
He wanted Jonah to go
to Nineveh.

He knew how to stop Jonah.

God sent a BIG storm!

The storm and wind were strong!

All the men on the boat were scared.

But not Jonah!

He was asleep in the boat.

The men went to see Jonah.

"Wake up!" they all shouted.

Jonah woke up.

"Help us, Jonah!

Talk to your God.

Ask him what we should do.

We are scared," they all said.

Jonah knew what to do.

He thought, *I cannot run from God.*

Jonah told the men,

"Throw me into the water.

Then the storm and the wind

will be quiet."

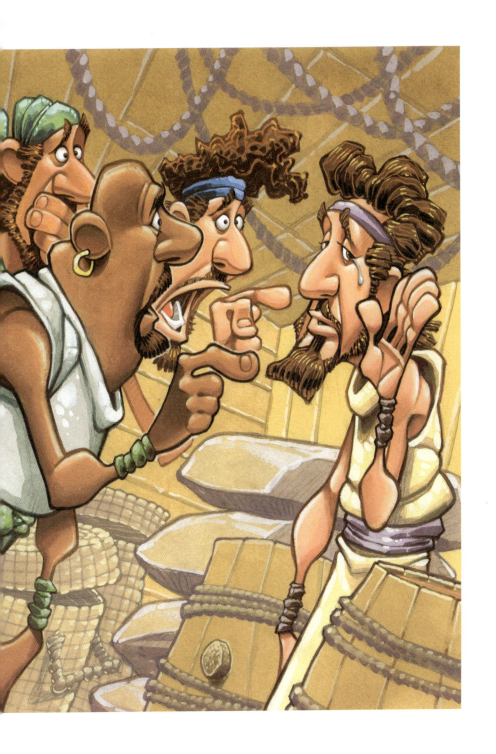

The men were scared.

But they did what Jonah said.

Jonah fell into the water

and went down,

down,

down …

Jonah fell deep into the sea.

God sent a huge fish

to catch Jonah when he fell!

Down Jonah went …

right into the mouth of the huge fish.

GULP!

Jonah was in the big fish for three days and three nights. Jonah prayed and prayed, "I am sorry, God. I am ready to do my job."

So God told the big fish to spit Jonah out!

Jonah landed on the shore.

He landed on dry land,

right where he needed to be.

Then God said to Jonah again,

"Go to Nineveh.

Tell the people about me.

Tell the people to be good!"

Jonah said, "OK, God. I will go."

Jonah told the people
in Nineveh about God.
The people believed Jonah.
They wanted to know more
about God.
God was happy with Nineveh,
and God was happy with Jonah!